A Twist of Lime Street

NEW AND SELECTED POEMS

Eddie Gibbons

To Anne,

with best wishes,

Eddie.

July 2013.

Red Squirrel Press

First published in the UK in 2013 by
Red Squirrel Press
Briery Hill Cottage
Stannington
Morpeth
Northumberland
United Kingdom
NE61 6ES
www.redsquirrelpress.com

Red Squirrel Press is distributed by Central Books
and represented by Inpress Ltd.
www.inpressbooks.co.uk

Cover by author

A CIP catalogue record is available from The British Library.

ISBM: 978-1-906700-62-1

Printed by Martins the Printers
Sea View Works
Spittal
Berwick upon Tweed
United Kingdom
TD15 1RS

EDDIE GIBBONS' first three poetry collections, *Stations of the Heart* (1999), *The Republic of Ted* (2003), and *Game On!* (2006), were published by Thirsty Books, Edinburgh. *Why She Flew to Barcelona* (2010) was published by Calder Wood Press, Dunbar. His previous collection, *What They Say About You* (2010), published by Leamington Books, Edinburgh, was shortlisted for the Poetry Section, Scottish Book of the Year Awards, 2011.

Eddie was a prize winner in the Inaugural Edwin Morgan International Poetry Competition, 2008. He was a regional judge for the Faber/Ottakar's National Poetry Competition, 2000 & 2001.

Acknowledgments

Thanks to John Smith of Aberdeen City Council, Douglas W. Gray of *Koo Press*, to Helena Nelson of *Happenstance Press*, to Eleanor Livingstone of *Stanza*, to Sheila Wakefield and Kevin Cadwallender of *Red Squirrel Press*, to *Birlinn/Polygon Press*, to Gideon Calder, and to Claire Askew of *One Night Stanzas* for including some of these poems in their anthologies.

Further thanks to Les Murray of *Quadrant Magazine*, Richard Price of *painted/spoken*, Jennie Renton of *The Scottish Book Collector*, Sally Evans of *Poetry Scotland*, and to the editors of *BBC Radio Scotland, Capital Radio, Sky TV, Northwords Now, Pushing Out the Boat, The Scotsman, Cutting Teeth, Read Raw, Spume, Snakeskin, Textualities, Football Poets, Writers for Libraries, Boo! Magazine* and *One Night Stanzas* for showcasing individual poems in their various media. Thanks also to Vicky Dawson of Yeadon's Booksellers, where I am currently Writer in Residence.

for Todd McEwen and Seán Bradley

'Oh, yeah, I'll tell you something,
I think you'll understand...'

Lennon / McCartney
I Want to Hold Your Hand

and for Barbara, Jennifer and Florian.

Contents

Suite: Silver Song

From *Game On!*

New Poems

Radiant Junctions
(Liverpool Lime Street, 1938)
for Steven Scholes and Peter Hart

Rain makes a river of reflections. Headlight beams shine this street to a glassy sheen. Windows glow with hearth-like invitation, hinting at some sweet delights unseen.

Trams ferry their freight through cobblestone tides. My father and mother could be in this picture: holding scholar tickets, seen upstairs on the Number Six, heading home from a day at the seaside, the circus, the flicks.

A foreground clock reads five past four. Back of the tick, back of the tock, streets are chock-a-block with characters: department stores and market stalls are stacked with stories from the Mersey Docks and Laughter Board.

Later, night will wash the sky of colour and daub these bars with a rosy flush. Tunes will flow into evening air, all lyrical and lush. This is a painted city, a written city, a spoken city: speech bubbles up where two figures pass. The craic fizzes up through pavement cracks.

History rides on tramline tracks: the East Lancs laid four years before, a road not yet travelled by Matt Busby, who will line up with Liddell in Liverpool red this season.

The Munich debacle is on the horizon: Chamberlain's infamous *Peace In Our Time.*

The last rays of hope shine from the cobbles. We know what's coming around the corner, what's approaching over the border. Crossing the junctions of our own lives, we pay no heed that the clock now reads one minute to midnight.

Stations of the Heart

And it Was

Was a time inside my time I dwelled beneath the twin-bird towers. Many youths with voices came from the hollows underground. Women walked stiletto streets which shone when rain fell all around. And in the air were aeroplanes and on the sea were ships. Was a time that was my time when bright were eyes the long day down. When curvy girls in giggle clusters tripped the pulse and sang the heart. Was in the town that was my town and I was young upon the world. And my brother called me brother and my sisters shone with dreams. Friends I had with many faces and they upped me in my downs. Was a river city bred me, buoyed me in my flood of years, my fears: those crystal chandeliers. And all around were shops and houses. On the road were many buses. *Hark!* the Herald Angels sang. *Come on you Reds!* my father cried. And the ice cream van was holy and my granny tied the knot. Brightly shone the candled chapel. Father, Son and Holy Smoke. In the room where childhood slumbered walls were four and future-facing. And the cup was on the saucer. In the grate a fire burned. Spooky Jesus smiled upon me and the walls were thick with saints. Bastards robbed my Granny's meter. Turned her over twice times three. God was in the television. Grandma had his autograph. One, the lone child down the alley. Two cathedrals linked by Hope Street. Three, the Graces on the seafront. Four, the misty Cast Iron Shore. And the smoke was in the chimney and the rent was never paid. And my father held my mother and he whispered *Love Me Do*. And my tea was on the table and he always shone our shoes. In our hearts glowed little candles, filled us with an inner light. And a lifetime sped before us, passed us by before we knew. And my mother died of fright in the night. I was naked on the stairs when the midnight call came through.

How It Will Be

You will think of her
less and less,
although you'll think
no less of her.

These thoughts, though few,
remain the strongest.
What you lose
stays with you longest.

A Liverpool Villanelle

A city has no boundaries.
It travels where its offspring roam.
My thoughts now shape what once shaped me.

Old clipper ships and slavery
are storylines in dusty tomes.
A city has no boundaries.

Twin talismans of heraldry
keep vigil on the Liver domes.
My thoughts now shape what once shaped me.

Black buildings grimed by industry,
where streets are streams of rusting chrome.
A city has no boundaries.

A boom-time town in 'sixty-three,
as frothy as the Mersey foam.
My thoughts now shape what once shaped me.

Then shiny times, with poetry:
the Cavern's worldwide metronome.
A city has no boundaries.

Now Thatcher's plague-years legacy
has left it like some ransacked Rome.
My thoughts now shape what once shaped me.

My heart still beats, though distantly,
for that far place I still call home.
A city has no boundaries.
My thoughts now shape what once shaped me.

Consider the Lily

I dream of Aunty Lily
back in 1963,
prior to Larkin's ditty
and the Rutles' first LP.

She dated Paul McCartney
(or so she said to me)
but he never came for tea
in her flat in Wavertree.

She wore highheels and lippy
as red as St. John's shirt.
She shaked the hippyhippy
in her minimini skirt.

Stomping in the Cavern,
twisting in the Sink,
gyrating in the Grafton
and posing in the Pink.

Lily smoked her Woodies
on long Locarno nights
and glimpses of her sussies
started many horny fights.

My darling Aunty Lily
was almost 23,
she gave me Wrigley's chewy
and let me watch TV.

I remember Lily:
so light, so flit, so flirt,
so feminine, so filly,
so frilly underskirt.

And I was small and happy
in 1963.
I loved my Aunty Lily
and Lily she loved me.

Epilepigram for the Cisco Kid

The shock stopped me
in my 10-year-old tracks:
a plump old biddy
jammed and jazzed
to the floor, poleaxed by a fit.

I thought it was a form of
pavement-jiving
for the over-fifties.

An urban voodoo
working on the neurons:
her handbag reeling
like a football rattle,
her floral frock
jitter-bugging
in its electric twitch.

Jolting synapses
spun her spiderwise
into a shambles,
pinned like a bug
in its whirl.

Being The Kid,
I rode to the shops
to buy some caps
for my Colt 45
to put her
out of her misery.

When I got back
the woman had gone.

Kirkby Comanches
for sure,
I thought,

as I headed West
across the endless
redbrick prairies
of Lancashire.

Jesse James Joyce

The day's been as glum as a poet's accountant.
A little more adventure wouldn't go amiss,
so I'll saddle-up my poems
and head 'em all out West...

I'll be The Lone Rhymer,
gunning for maverick metaphors
and vigilante verses
with silver-bullet six-shooters.
(Who was that masked muse?)

Or dressed up all in black atop a palamino,
catching Davy Crockett's hat
falling at the Alamo.

Poem, poem on the range...

Where desperado couplets
dressed in ponchos
and sombreros
pass out on tequilas
in El Paso haciendas.

I'll be Jesse James Joyce
with a Stevie Smith and Wesson
ambushing the Pony Express
for Seamus Heaney First Editions.

I'll pow-wow with Cochise
inside a ring of fire,
trading buffalo hides
for bows of burning gold
and arrows of desire.

Several boys named Sioux
will jostle for a view,
Sitting Bull will have to stand
to see above the crowd

as I read aloud
Custer's Last Stanza.

Then I'll scalp Ted Hughes
and become the first Poet Lariat.

The Marginal Fields

The bottom's dropped out of the barrel again,
and the gravy train has been derailed at Aberdeen.

It's the downside of the fossil fuel boom,
the five-year lull when all the graphs
plunge off the page.

The rigs are built to stand the Hundred-Year-
Wave: the surfer's wet wet dream.

But mortgages sink faster
than gangsters in concrete Reeboks,
and here's me mid-pool,
no snorkel in sight.

So its back to the doledrums;
the onshore survival course:
stopped cheques,
coffee mornings with the bailiffs,
valentines from the procurator fiscal,
sheriff's officers
and the hydro heavy gang.

I'm holding the fort
until the markets are buoyant
and the marginal fields
surrender their yield.

Meanwhile, I've decided
on the Writer's life:
I'm translating Yevtushenko
into Doric and selling the texts
at reserve games at Pittodrie.

It's the job security that attracts me.

Black as Jazz

Let's slip into our shadow-selves again,
and haunt the umber hours until dawn.

We'll seek the hidden raptures down below
the neon-painted pavements of this town.

We'll slide into some room where tunes will plumb
the dark delights of freeform jazz and soul.

And in those minutes we will be alive
to rhythms from a deeper inner tide.

Our skins will turn to mottled midnight tones,
like moonlit snow dissolving over coals.

And should the music bind us to its time,
we'll trade these truant moments for our days.

To live beyond this world where white hours pass:
the continent of night is black as jazz.

Killing Time

I'm drinking alone, and living dangerously,
reading poetry in this skinhead teuchter bar.
I'm reading poems by Polish writers, dispatches
from the ghettos: Krakow, Warsaw; 1944.

It looks as if I'm killing time but I'm really
reconstructing it, fifty heartbeats to a page.

There's been a lack of craic all evening.
The barmaid's just attained the 7th level of boredom.
This Caffrey's is cloudy but it's clearing slowly.
The lottery draw's on the video screen.

But my mind's on the book and the scenes it describes:
smoke, gunfire, bombs; the heart's alarms.

The barmaid's eyes are as dull as the decor.
A punter takes a shine to her but gets rebuffed.
Just as well, he slurs, *the only thing that's hard
these days is my luck.*

A Prince among men is wailing from the jukebox:
Tonight I'm gonna party like it's 1999.

It's a song on the end of an epoch.
And there's a song on the end of the world
in the city of Warsaw beneath my thumb, where
a man is writing a book in the ruins of his local pub.
The decor here is frost and swastikas.
The barmaid's shoes are buried in snow.

The man is alone in the smoke and the shadows.
Downing his dregs, he closes the book
on himself. He takes his leave of no-one.
He enters the night. The night enters him.

www.coma

I logged on
as *Global Villager,*
spent hours in
an on-line chat group
really connected
with people
from all over
the world.

Energised,
I went to the pub
but left early
to avoid
my next-door
neighbours.

.

The Season in the Room

She's been here again,
all the signs speak of her:
the landscape draped across the sofa,
the satin petals cushioned on the chair.

The trace of lacework haunting the settee
is the ghost of embroidery.

Her stock-in-trade filigree
has left its shallow signature.
Yes, she has been here.

Tonight, when eyes are hostage to sleep,
the sound of scissors will snip the silence.

A threaded flower will bloom
and a season's colours
will seep through her fingers.

Tomorrow, a small rectangle of spring
will be hung on the living room wall.

Man on the Moon

In the street beside the Lemon Tree
a giggle of tipsy tourists stop
abruptly. One of them, a girl
no older than her tongue, raises
an arm and a finger and tickles
the chin of the moon.
HELLO, MOON she purrs
MOON, HELLO.

On the pavement by the Prince
a drunken pundit tipples
topsy-turvy into a puddle.
He cuddles his liquid pillow
and serenades the face beside him:
HELLO, MOON he croons
MOON, HELLO.

Soon every strip of neon,
every registration plate,
every sign and signal
up and down the town
is beaming and blaring
and every tongue is twisted
'round the words:
HELLO, MOON they chorus
MOON, HELLO.

Sick of all this lunacy,
this moonacy, I drive away
to meet my daughter at her work.
My radio queries:
Andy, have you heard about this one..?
It's one of her favourites. Hers.
My daughter's. My only daughter's.

And me, her only father. I have no son.
I have a moon. My own moon.
I orbit her, she orbits me.
What we share is light-
heartedness and the sure and certain
belief that REM will save the world.

This no sooner thought than she's there,
stood stock-still in front of me.
Wide-eyed, mouth agape. Moonstruck.
Her tongue rises above the white horizon
of her teeth:
HELLO, MOON she murmurs
MOON, HELLO.

Aeons later she disentrances
and I come to her senses:

Thanks for waiting, Dad, and did
you see the moon tonight?
And Dad, did you say
HELLO?

The Gap

'Here's where old Gibbons jumped from, Robinson.'
—Weldon Kees *(Aspects of Robinson)*

Robinson at the scene. The bridge. The span. The vertical drop.
A fall from gracelessness, evidently. Robinson musing over
personal items: a wallet, a watch, a ring, a Visa. Neatly piled
at the point of departure. The view from the edge: a breath-
taking vista. Metres of air. Fathoms of water. The gap: at a
push the depth of ten buses turned on their noses. He stepped
off the wagon and into the drink, his brinkmanship trumped.
A slip of the tongue twisting fail into fall? Or jilt into jump?
A tug, a dredger churning the bottom. Robinson lobbing a
stone overboard and clocking the time 'til the stone takes
a soaking. The gutting-shed stench cutting into his nostrils.
Nauseous odours of petrol and diesel swim up from the river.
Robinson, clueless, turns up his collar and turns on his heels
to track down a diner. A burger, a Jack, a slim panatella to
bridge the gap and fuel the enigma.

Portrait of Ana Dali

Ana Dali, Salvador's sister,
shown here in an ominous frock,
eloped with an amorous easel
to the melting apartment block.
She waves through a hole in a mirror
sewn into her brother's smock.
As she drinks the breeze from the Pyrenees
Time drips from the village clock.

Her pigtails stretch from her window
to Cadaques and the port of Bilbao.
Over sun-speltered Andalucia
through measureless meadows of cows.
Her lemonade has developed amnesia.
Her maracas engage in a row.
Her Mercedes Benz is ablaze at both ends.
She is wearing a watch that says *NOW!*

An orangepeel twist forms her fingers,
her mouth is a door left ajar.
The Atlantic cascades from her shoulders
where Cervantes tilts at the stars.
Her nose is the shape of the town of Cadiz.
Her cheeks form the base of a vase.
Her hair is coiffured in a whirlwind of birds.
Her eyes are Flamenco guitars.

Acrylic skies frame her figure,
painted with luminous grace.
She gazes at astral horizons
in the infinite sadness of space.
She sits in a gilded garden,
a paranoid, marigold place.
She is humming a tune
to the Catalan moon
through a veil of vermilion lace.

Stuff Pythagoras

The affair that is hot news
is equal to the fun of the affairs
with the other two guys

he said
obtusely

But this is one triangle
that won't be eternal —
it's a sine of the times

she replied
as she flew off at a tangent

Out of Dates

40
goes to Tesco's
Pulls out
a packet
labelled
LOVE

(He'd forgotten
the flavours:
*Pure & Tender /
Raw & Flirty*)

He sighs
and shelves it

The label reads:

Best before
30

I Look Up

A sudden gust flusters
the leaves of the book.
I look up from the poem.
The room has changed.
You are in it.

Your face is the same
as when I last saw it,
though now obscured
by another man's shadow.

Your voice chimes softly
down the years
and whispers past me
on to other rooms.

Always the traveller,
you were just a tourist
in my heart,
collecting souvenirs
for your Love Affair
Museum.

A wet-dream dealer
in stilettos and rouge,
always flirting with mirrors
and smiling at strangers.

I picture you with others,
at airports,
planes lifting all around you.

Sometimes I see you
in slippers, at stoves;
a bedsit refugee,
letterless and lonely.

A sudden gust flusters
the leaves of the book.

I look down at the page.
The poem has changed.
You are in it.

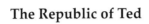

The Republic of Ted

My Boss, the Sea

In the grey estates of Industry
all outlooks are bleak. Windows
seldom show more than the factory
opposite; a dirty apex of corrugated misery.
Often the view is a drab brick wall.

But in this new job one of the windows
looks out on the sea. It is a small rectangular
blessing, a keyhole full of weather, sending
reports of seagulls, currents and clouds.

Now and then, when I look up
from the universal oblong of Windows 98
I can sometimes see a tiny red ship take an age
to traverse the length of the window ledge.

When I turn back to my screen
my boss is usually at my shoulder,
branding me a dreamer who should pay
more attention to desktop icons and less
to maritime meanderings.

So I continue drawing details on my screen.
When the prints are issued they will be sent
to the client, who will build a huge red ship
and send it sailing, tiny, past my window.

Frames

He met her
at the art gallery.
Made eyes at her
across a Caravaggio.
Saw her framed
against a Miro.
Watched her glide along
an avenue of Monets.

She saw him standing
like a prick
between two Pollocks.

Why Buses Come in Threes

The first bus leaves the depot on time,
picks up all the passengers
and drops them all off.

The second bus leaves the depot on time,
but now has fewer passengers to pick up
and so catches up with the first bus.

The third bus leaves from no depot.
It has no driver.
It glows a venomous green
and is made of pure spite.

Confession

Forgive me, father, for I have rhymed coat with boat and loving with longing. Believe me when I say it was never my intention to commit such crimes. How things came to such a pretty pass is hard to recount, my being from stout working-class stock— a son of toil, a grain of earth salt. I was a redbrick-and-rain child with holy socks and grazed knees. Please take into account the fact that I once beat the shit out of Rayo Graham that night his gang jumped me behind the chippy. He hit me first but I felt no pain. Adrenaline is the one true drug. I shrugged when he fell to the ground for the final time and I looked around at faces etched with fear and respect. I expect no clemency for writing poetry —it's a heinous act— but consider the fact that I lifted that tenner from the sweetshop counter and went back later for the evening paper and brassed-out the shopkeeper's dirty looks. Did I spend it on books? Like heck I did— that ten quid bought a ticket for Inter in the Kemlyn Road, three pints of bitter in the Arkle pub and a ten-bob sub to my brother to pay the Tally and his fares to work. I never shirk my duties where family's concerned— every penny I earned went to Mum, Dad and wife, and what I had left was a short-change life which needed supplementing somehow, so I turned to crime, petty not pretty. I kept my hand in someone else's pockets. Learned the thrill of a ransacked till, the pleasure in parting the leather of a pilfered purse and rolling a wad in my fevered mitt. It's a hit no drug can ever match: like lifting the latch of a shut-up shop, sweeping the ciggies into a sack, then vaulting the wall to the alley out back without alarming a dog or a cat. Father, I know you'll forgive me for that, but not my cack-handed knack of pummelling prose into poem-sized pots. Bring out your cross, your sceptre and mitre and save this poor sinner from robbing the metre.

Schrödinger's Cat Flap

The cat flap is closed.
Is the cat inside or outside?

The pessimist's answer:
The cat is inside, curled up on the rug.

The optimist's answer:
The cat is outside under a truck.

Schrödinger's answer:
The cat is both inside and outside
at the same time.

The poet's answer:
Who cares if
the cat is sat on the mat
or the cat is splat and flat?

The world is all imagining:
the rhyme's the thing

Shopping Forecast

The Shopping Forecast issued by the Dole Office
at 19:30 on Thursday 8th June.

There are warnings of Sales in Fraser's,
Debenhams, Esslemont and Macintosh.

The general Shopping List at 13:00 —

Iceland, North Utsire, South Utsire.
10p off at Iceland, while stocks last.
Lurpak £1.06 decreasing 5 or 6p
by 13:00 tomorrow.
North it's dearer, south it's dearer.

Faeroes, Cromarty Co-op.
Fisherman's Friends reduced
to tears. Automatic Lighthouse
on the blink. 40-watt
lightbulbs sold out.

German Bite, Biscuit, Thin as Air.
Strudels, Hobnobs, 5p off.
Peckish, becoming famished 1 or 2.
Decreasing 3 or 4
dress sizes.
Gail, forced, ate.

Isle of Jura, Baileys, Rhum.
70p off 70cl.
Westerly, veering uncertainly.
Becoming paralytic after 6 or 7.
Occasional slurring.
Dribble.
Poorly later.

Hiking, Base Rate, Robber Bank.
Variable, becoming high.
Extortionate for a time.
APR 20 or 30.
Mastercard and Visa low.
Hard rain.
Overdraft increasing 100%.
Poor.

Viking, Forties, GSOH.
Low, 100 miles south of Shetland.
WLTM Siren or Silkie
No mermaids.
Rising northwesterly
in anticipation.

That is the end of the Shopping Forecast.

Suite: Silver Song

Vernacular

What you notice first
about my father
is his spectacular
vernacular:

the way he rounds
his diphthongs is sound
as a pound. His diction is
guttural with a nasal twang.

That night he sang
Please Release Me
at the Labour Club
is karaoke folklore,
though at the time
he called it *doing a turn.*

He'll drop his aitches
at the drop of a hat,
knock his vowels stone
cold flat and build
a sentence with syllabic
slabs as thick as doorsteps
on a Toxteth terrace.

His accent is one third Irish,
one third English
and one third catarrh;
his speech sounds like
an untuned guitar.

It's hard to avoid his
adenoidal lingo
when he's ordering
bevvies down at the Bingo
or telling me jokes
whenever I phone.

His voice sounds like laughter.
His voice sounds like home.

Camera Obscura
(A trip to Edinburgh, 2002)

Scaling four flights of stairs,
we stopped at each level
for my father to catch
his breath and rest
his tired *Edinburgh Legs.*

In time we caught up
with the others
and entered the darkroom
of the Camera Obscura.

We gathered, séance-like,
around the plinth
where a pinhole and mirrors
projected the view
from the top of the tower:

the Castle, where tourists
trod their tiny paths;
the City, where toytown traffic
inched its way down Princes Street.

Then Calton Hill, the Firth of Forth
and Arthur's Seat.

We watched, like Greek Gods
might have done from Olympus,
small lives in motion
beneath our fingers.

Is this what death is:
a trick of the light?

And later, past holograms,
mirrors, light's hocus-pocus,
a pinhole camera rendered
my father's upside-down face:
the fear of his x-rays sharply in focus.

Don't Phone From Work

Don't dial nine
for an outside line
to ask the Ward Sister
if he's any better.

The only words
she will utter
are *prostate, cancer*
and *pneumonia.*

Then a quiet insistence
to scoop you hollow—
Fly down today,
don't wait 'til tomorrow.

Show your new face
to the office floor—
set in a grimace
wild, bewildered, raw.

The Man in the Sack

On Sunday mornings
you'd take me to the Pier Head
to see Punch punch Judy
and watch the ferries waltz
to Wallasey.

I'd gasp as waves
rocked the Floating Dock,
feel faint at the sight
of the drop glimpsed
between slats.

Crowds of men
in old-fashioned hats
formed a ring around
a man in a sack
shackled by chains.

He became a blind
Dervish, his straining
and grunting scaring
the life out of
dozens of kids.

He twisted and feinted,
grappled and swerved
as if wrestling a demon,
while we shouted
Come on, you can do it!

Fifty years later
I have to unravel
your twisted blankets,
to free your tangled
catheter tube.

You're wrestling with
a different demon:
I stand helpless,
chanting lowly
Come on, you can do it!

Remembering the Fish

Receiving a smile
of rare recognition,
I chatted about
my journey from Scotland.

His evening meal arrived
on a trolley —
fish and chips,
ice cream and jelly.

He fumbled with
his knife and fork,
so I cut up his fish,
fed him four mouthfuls
before he was finished.

I stayed for five hours
although he was sleeping,
fussed with his blankets,
adjusted his pillows;
steeped in the silence
between his breathings,
turned off the light
as I was leaving.

The following day,
astoundingly lucid,
he claimed he saw no-one
the previous evening.

I joked that I'd walked
from Aberdeen,
and he couldn't recall
I'd even been.

He chewed the thought over
for several minutes.

Oh, yes,
you're right—
I remember the fish.

The Domino Effect

One small thing
leans on another,

grows into something
no one can gather
from the first signs
often looked over,

like that blank tile
I placed that day
we played our last
game together—

you the child,
I the father.

When your spots
added up
to double sixes,

no magic or hexes
could place the dies
back in their boxes—

the ones, the twos,
in natural order
with no wild numbers

to bring such disorder
as the terrorist cells
rioting inside you.

Dire Morphine (i)

I phoned the hospital.
The Ward Sister answered:

He's had a bad night
but he's comfortable now.

I'm thinking of flying down
again tomorrow.

Yes, you should do that,
but due to the drugs
he probably won't know
who you are.

Maybe not,
but I know who he is.

Dire Morphine (ii)

I arrive unrecognised—
a stranger in his room.

He's taken apart
his diamorphine machine,
severed the pulsing artery tube.

His hands are agitating—
he's pulling tissues
out of a box, as if expecting
to pluck out a rabbit.

His eyes stare beyond me:
his mind is fifty years younger,
his face is fifty years older.
His mouth is set in a scowl.

His hands are still working
on the transmission line,
assembling endless unseen cogs.

He kisses my sister on the cheek
and says my mother's name.

The room is full of ghosts.

He's vexed and I'm fucked
if I'm going to stand for it,
so I get the nurse
to change his dosage.

He is calmer now, though
I'm more distraught—

his hands had shown signs of life—
signs of unseen cogs at work.

Double Act

We've always been
peas in a pod, me and you.
I'm the Toshack to your Keegan,
the Rush to your Dalglish.

I see your smile
when I look in a mirror,
catch myself miming
all your gestures.

But one half of us
is now half of himself
and any day now
I'll be left on the bench,

adrift from the source
of a lifetime's laughter;
doomed to the role
of a solo performer—

St. John without Hunt,
Owen without Fowler—
out on a limb—
the lost lone striker.

What Not to Buy Him

His seventh week in hospital—
still no positive results.
We're hesitantly optimistic.

I'm alone with my father.
He leans towards me and whispers:

Rita was in the consultant's room
for half an hour this morning.
What do you think they said to her?

Don't buy him any LPs?

A1, A3, A4

Standard sizes
I use every day
for printing drawings.

The area diminishes
as the number increases.

A1, A3, A4 —
the hospital wards
my father's been through,
his failing health

turning him
from portrait to landscape,

decreasing the borders
of the Republic of Ted —

Those walls.
That door.
This bed.

Dance the Night Away

Wearied by the bedside vigils,
we decided one night
to push the boat out—
to celebrate
instead of pre-mourn you.

We played your favourite
music, sang the old songs
and danced until
night became day,

while the boat of your bed
drifted slowly away.

Beyond Language

The Angel of Death appeared
in a light blue shirt.
He was wearing glasses.
He had a clipboard in his hand
and a badge that read
Macmillan Nurse.

He sat down
and gave my father
his inside story
in a measured
matter-of-fact way.

The Angel had kind eyes
and a calm voice,
and I realised

he was The Angel of Life
with a tough job to do.

When he'd finished he left
his calling card and said
If there's anything

My father turned to me and

Man of the Cloth

His final morning
of consciousness—

the nurse came in
to salve his crusted tongue
with swabs soaked in alcohol.

The first was whisky,
with he sucked with relish.

The second was Pernod,
which made him smile.

The nurse called in a colleague
to see the look of pleasure
on Ted's face.

She had a bed cloth
folded over her arm.

When the nurse asked Ted
if he wanted anything else,
he pointed to the bed cloth
and said: *Soak that!*

The Laughing Man

Did I sit beside that bed
for hours on end,
watching the clock's
grim reckoning
and the light's slow fading
draw its shadows
down the curtains?

Was there a catheter, a drip,
water that could not be sipped?

Was that my own father there,
or nobody I ever knew?
Was that face my father's face,
those hands the ones I'd held?

Those vacant eyes,
that open mouth—
that was never him.

But where is he—
the laughing man
I used to know?

Where is the boy he used to be?

The soldier of Trieste?
That upright man reduced to this?

A Single Drop

I took the top off
his eye-drop bottle,
washed it out
and filled it with water.

I placed a single drop
on his tongue.
It choked him.

His body was beyond
my caring,

and I found myself
choking on that single
drop of love.

Nil-Nil by Mouth

Palliative?
What does that mean?

It means he can't take food or fluids—
he'll choke on a crumb or a drop.
The drip's turned off.

That evening, his last before the coma,
we draped his blankets in Liverpool colours.

Holding his hand, me and my brother
watched with him our last match together—
Auxerre away in the UEFA.

It was goalless when he gestured
for the nurses to bring the toilet.

Robert and I went for a coffee.
The nurses brought that pointless potty—
nothing had passed through his mouth for days.

He was living inside a morphine haze—
his eyes were open while he slept
and a lifetime passed between each breath.

It was still nil-nil when we returned.
Nil by mouth. No last words.

AGM/DNR

Present:
Self, siblings.

Absent:
Hope.

Subject:
Father.

Business:
To decide whether attempts
should be made to resuscitate
the subject should the drugs
cause a heart attack.

Staff Nurse Pamela
provided tea and biscuits.

Death took the minutes.

Speed Bumps

They're a curse!
said the ambulance driver
as we crested the seventh
tarmac wave and you winced.

I took your hand,
caressed your brow —

It's OK, we're nearly home.

The paramedic next to me
said they'd complained
endlessly to the council —

It's poor sick sods
like your Dad that suffer.

I nodded as we shunted
the last bump
and the motion made
you sigh one final time —

your breath rising
and falling
like wind over the ocean.

The Weight

How far is it now, Ted?
Not far, Joe, not far, mate.

They're halfway between Woolfall Heath
and Broadgreen. Nightime, 1938,
halfway along a three-mile route;
Ted in his hand-down shoes,
Joseph in his scuffed-up boots.

They passed the Page Moss terminus
too late for any bus, too skint to hail
a cab. No ambulance in sight tonight—
Shanks's pony is the only way to go.

It hurts, Ted.
I know Joe, I know.

This is Joe's final journey, Ted's longest
trek. Joseph is on Ted's back, racked
by pneumonia. Joseph is twelve, Ted,
a year his junior. Joe is heavy, but
he's his brother.

At home, their fretting mother
ties knots in her rosary
for every pavement slab between
Woolfall Heath and Broadgreen.

At Death's Door

He left the room
but the door was closed.
Where did he go?

Death took him.
You saw it.
You were there.

I saw nothing
that was not
there before.

But something changed…

Yes, I remember now.
I heard him breathing.
Then I heard nothing.

Death is a silent thief.

I kissed his forehead.
It was cold.
Cold in minutes.

Death takes everything.

So Death caused his dying?

No, Life did that.
Dying is a lifetime's work.
Life closes the door.

And what does Death do?
Death slams it shut.

A Penny for the Guy

Every bonfire night
we'd pinch
your old shirts,
shoes and pants
to dress the Guy
for his moment
of fame,
then watch him
disappear
in flames.

Now you, too,
have gone out
in a blaze of glory.

We told the story
to the papers—

your *mori,*

our *memento*—

Small Ads:
Deaths;
received an invoice
from *The Echo.*

All you were,
all you did,
and a penny change
from fifteen quid.

Reunion

I'm handed the casket
containing your ashes.
It weighs the same
as I did as an infant.

Kneeling, I lower you
into the ground
where my mother was
buried nine years before,
completing this final
tender reunion.

Pressing gently,
I move you toward her,
as once you pressed gently
lover to lover,
producing the hands
that now tremble above you.

I stand to face
your gene congregation
and read the poem
that choked in my throat
at each rehearsal
for seven days passing
but now rings clear
as a church bell chiming.

All heads are bowed,
a last prayer is whispered:
we walk, diminished,
into the future.

The Day After

I looked out on Helsby Hill
each day above your windowsill.
I watched in shadow, rain and sleet;
morning, afternoon and night.

The day before your day of days
the hill stood in a drizzle haze.
And when the paramedics came
we took that last short journey home.

Today I'm here and you are gone,
on Helsby Hill I stand alone
and watch the clouds go drifting by
beneath the endless empty sky.

The day is fresh and bright and clear,
the hospital's just over there—
and now I wish I could contrive
to be back there, with you alive.

Game On!

The Sweet Silver Song
I.M. Ted Gibbons (1927-2003)

Rita, Keith and I are in the British Legion
to choose a menu for the wake.

We're at the end of the long bar.
It's early afternoon and the staff are busily
taking stock to the sound of music
piped through speakers.

Rita points to the far end of the bar —

*Dad's photo is pinned to the obituary board
if you want to take a look.*

I know it's the one where he's sitting at a table
wearing his green Liverpool away shirt.
He's grinning, offering a pint to the camera.

The instant I stand in front of the photo,
smiling back at him, a shower of silver words
rains from the speaker above my head:

*'When you walk through a storm,
hold your head up high
and don't be afraid of the dark.
At the end of the storm there's a golden sky
and the sweet silver song of the lark…'*

This tune, our bonding song down all the seasons,
gives me my life's one holy moment,
washing away my grief.

I stand in baffled silence, innocent as an infant,
reunited with my father until the last note fades.

I walk on,
a sinner
ambushed by angels.

The Starlight Cup

Two coats are best for posts. The bar defined by stars.
The ball, a small elusive animal at twilight.

Two kids are best for this, this game without a name;
this thrall, this all-consuming spell of moonlight.

Hours are devoured. Dark is the park.
In a blink the sink estate fades from view.

Sounds are muffled, baffled in the lee of trees.
Only one stark bark pierces through.

The Dream Team plays deep into the night; no fright
will scare them aware, shake their belief

that there's no relegation from imagination—
nothing in the street can beat this wakeful sleep.

The prize they win tonight is theirs to keep.

Bottle Job

I was a toddler
when I first kicked
a ball —it was
a beauty— it flew
from my bootee
and knocked
my brother's bottle
out of his toothless
gob. Waving my bib,
I did a ruthless
streak past his cot,
then dribbled his bottle
around the settee
and thought:
this game's for me!

Football Associations

Early inklings of crucial connections:
the bicycle pump, the casey adaptor,
the screw-in stud; all were somehow
connected with mud, the true element
of childhood, along with blood.

The pump connected to the ball.
The stud connected to the boot.
The boot connected with someone's head:
another little bleeder bled.

Saturdays were Matinees in Picture Houses:
Swizzles, Love Hearts, sugar-coated Disneys;
then out into the drizzle and a dash for the bus
to the playing fields, your kit wrapped in a towel.

Then, almost overnight, the game changed.
It was as if your brain had been rewired
to your trousers, all previous connections severed.

Lumps appeared everywhere,
especially in blouses.

All the houses
in your street became bordellos
of rioting hormones with nowhere to go.

I Am Curious Yellow was the show
which you hoped might have trailers
of the vital action to follow:

the flirt, the kiss, the fumble
on her parents' settee. But especially
the x-rated edits of carnal nights.

Hold your breath at the credits—
is your name up in lights?

Half-Time Haikus

nil-nil at the break
each team missed a penalty
empty nets both ends

ten thousand lighters
pass their flames to cigarettes
a terrace inhales

pie and bovril time
volcanic temperatures
scald our lips and tongues

the trannie's whisper
translates into whoops and shouts
rivals are losing

toilets overflow
bursting punters face the wall
thirty waterfalls

zipped-up trousers turn
scampering towards their seats
teams take to the pitch

Ritual

Some run on the pitch
for their first kick,
others touch the grass,
lift the hand to their mouths,
kiss a finger, bless
themselves, and this
is a sacrament, a wish
for assistance to assess
the flight of the toss,
the height of the pass,
the weight of the cross.

Football Matters
for Brian Webster

It mattered that some early-season Saturday
a butcher's shop would close at twelve, and a factory
klaxon release a greased and grimed assembly line
to their bicycles, Lambrettas and Reliant Robins.

It mattered that the toast was buttered and the tea
was strong enough to hold a goalpost, and that
the radiogram played *Orange Blossom Special*
at full throttle while the toasted cheese
melted the bacon's heart.

Saturdays assembled around the working men, who
hunched on Woodbined seats as football buses wound
along the threadbare streets of the far estates, reeling
the scarfed and rattle-roused spectators to the stadium.

Most bailed out at pubs along the thoroughfare:
The Rocket, The Sandon, The Cabbage Hall. Small boys sat
on steps, cradling bottled stout, not daring to set foot inside
to find their fathers in the hubbub of the shouting lounges,
the shrieking saloons.

When the jeaned and Brylcreemed masses left the
overflowing ashtrays and the dregs of Guinness glasses
to the tender care of barmaids, the pavements and the
roadways streamed towards the turnstiles and the choruses
chiming on the nicotine breeze.

The press and cram of people made islands out of motorcars
and wrecked the privet hedges of redbrick terraced houses.
A child's hand, held tight for fear of slipping from a father's
grasp, was securely gripped as any captain's hold around a
ribboned cup.

And this was the story and the match report for every game: he held his father's hand and his father led him to the ground where, sometimes on the stanchions, sometimes on his shoulders, his father raised him up like a trophy, like a glory.

Your Poems

This poem is abowt
your Boltons,
your Aberdeens,
your Celtics &
your Cardiffs.

But it's not about
your Rangerses,
your Wolveses,
your Heartses
or your Hamilton Academicalses.

It's not one of your *Novels* or your *Plays* —
it's one of your *Poems*.

Stand up if you hate this poem.
But if you like it, please enquire about the author—
Who Are Ya? Who Are Ya?
Are you McGonagall in disguise?

He will be flattered by your interest.

You might have a pop at the poem
if you think you're hard enough,
but it's always handbags at ten paces,
and you only win when you're singing.

The poem will have been disappointed with that last line.

But the poem knows the First Leg is a half of two games.
It's taking each line as it comes. It will go down to the wire
where the Fat Lady sings of parrots and moons.

It knows that 4-4-2 is 4 lines short of a sonnet
and realises that there's more than one effin Faber,
one effin Faber, there's more than one effin Faber.
And there's two Andy Gorams.

Sylvia Plath? You're having a laugh!

The poem was unsighted for that spelling error
in the first line, but think twice before giving it the elbow —
this baby's got *bouncebackability* — it will bite your leg off,
hit you with the soggy end and sell you a dummy,
you dummy.

But at the end of the day if it kept you away from
those stupid pundits then the poem done good.

Forensic

What happened here today
will melt into mythology,
and in the melancholy air
of some misty Saturday
the whistle now blowing
will come to symbolise
something precious lost.

There will be a demotion
of hopes; folklore and old
songs will be sewn together,
sung and told forever as
distant recollections,
grains of consolation
for the dark days ahead.

See, someone will say,
it's almost visible:
the scuff of grass
where he placed the ball—
the brief union
of boot and history
shooting into immortality.

The Virgin and the Goalie

He tipped her over the bar at a night club—

Keep the change, luv.

He ordered a highball, no ice,
due to his fear of slippery surfaces.

He was on the rebound, he said,
another long shot
had slipped through his fingers.

He had some extra time
to kill, so how would she fancy
being cradled in a safe pair of hands?

He thought he'd trapped her
but she back-heeled him
for a more striking partner.

He was too forward, she said,
and she didn't want to be handled
by someone out of his box.

He drank his bitter,
swallowed his pride,
and hit the streets.

She moved the goalposts.
He kept clean sheets.

Look Away Now

If you don't want to know the score.

The linesman's flagging, and so is your team.
A figure in black is haunting your dreams.

He's judge and jury of who is at fault.
The season will turn on this one result.

The banners are sagging. The chanting has stopped.
Your wife's disappeared while out at the shops.

A note on the table, a valediction,
a wedding ring pinned to the inscription.

The girl from your office has spilled the beans
to your wife on the phone, a bitter scene.

Your daughter's in bed with that prick next door.
He's brought all his Mates to show her the score.

Your son's away with friends out the back
giving him needle, they're having the crack.

Your doctor's report is crossing his desk,
affirming results from your screening test.

A penalty's given. A minute to go.
Look away now if you don't want to know.

Why She Flew to Barcelona

Love in the Time of Coreldraw

Once I would have laid a rosebud at your feet,
sent a scented missive in an envelope delivered
by a go-between; stood beneath your window
in a blizzard of snowdrops, hoping for a glimpse
of your shadow in the moonlight.

But times have altered the language of the heart.
The lexicon of longing is no longer written longhand,
with soaring serifs scribed in ink on beds of vellum,
but by illuminated texts on Ericssons and Vodafones,
and new-millennium lovers go Blackberry picking down
lanes of pay-and-go, past Oranges and Apple phones.

Once keystrokes onto paper kept the rhythm
of romance: ribbons bled red streams of yearning,
or keys rapped out the stuttering sentiments of
nervous suitors onto scented sheets of lavender,
which they sent, post-haste to beloveds
in lanes and streets and avenues.

These days my words to you are more mobile
and predictable: more to the pointer, more pithy,
more reducible, and so, my love, I offer you these
tokens on my part— my dingbats, my emoticons,
my clip-art heart.

Ripcord

It's the red-eyed Early Bird again today,
the pre-dawn flight, ABZ to LPL.

Drawn to your ward on the wings
of a jet; its engines throttling,

lifting and descending but leaving
me hovering at 20,000 feet,

surrounded by the endless stars
in their countless constellations,

backlit by the thin arc of sunrise
bathing the rim of the planet

in primordial light, suspending me
in this purgatory: the thought of you

dying expanding through my universe
like a parachute opening inside my lungs.

The First Time I Met Algebra

my first line of defence was to attack it
with anagrams; but *grab ale, a garble*, even
bare gal were not enough to cure the trauma.

My former fear was long division—
those Babel-towering numerals spoke
no language that I knew: I was number dumb.

My mathematics were derisory, my thematic
was prosody. No rosy future beckoned me
from the thorny bush of numeracy.

Algorithms gave me the blues.
Quadratics ruled the roots in schools.
Fractions made me fractious.

I was top of the form in despondency
until a classmate reminded me that
x and y are the last two letters of sexy.

So I wrote a sexy poem for her
about how an x wanted to get a y
between satin sheets of parentheses

but I received the same rejection as
my maths exam submission—
were you born stupid, or do you practice?

On my way home from school I noticed
a woman weeping by the railway station.
No need to guess. I knew: my maths teacher.

Twilight Talons

I swim in luminescence in my insulated room.

A book glows on my lap. The TV beams
its satellite streams back towards the moon.
Its reflection flickers on my windowpane.

My glow-worm world is protected by a thin
skin of science: the membrane of modern
magic repels the alchemy and spells of that
dark terrain beyond the pane.

The night is an enormous cave where
horn and tooth and claw conspire
to reap their crimson harvest.

Out there bats scrape the night with sonar,
owls scoop blood by beakfuls, hawks rake
their shrill reports across the moonless moors.
The sounds claw at the pane.

Darkness has wings, and the twilight talons,
out there where feather wreaks its vengeance on fur.

A small point of life drinks my light; a moth
wafts its way towards my reservoir of brightness,
to be impaled by a scything starling.

Only its thin pain between us.

Tête à Tate

This earnest lad with his Debenhams Diva
imagines himself a bristling bridegroom,
little knowing this relationship will stretch him
like a canvas to the limit, unaware
how much he'll fracture, or how quickly
love's lava cools from lover to hater, from
love her to *hate her*, from glider to Stuka—
how the lily fields turn into battlefields
and *yearn for her* becomes *Guernica*.

Modernist Love

Bored of the Modernists, he's trying
to hurry her to more erotic Movements.

She holds him back, entranced
by a vision of floating brides: the veils,
the trains, the faded bouquets. She mourns
the demise of everyone's marriages, guesses
romance dies in the kitchen, the laundry, et al.

He asks if she fancies a quick Chagall.

Vinnocence

Is it Van Goff, Van Gock or Van Go?
How do you say his name?

Do you cough it? Do you choke it?
Does it set your throat aflame?

I simply call him Vincent,
like that song by Don McLean.

Vincent the innocent,
patron saint of paint and pain.

In Vigil, Later

In junior school we took turns to be milk monitor,
braving brittle winter mornings to collect crates
from the playground and deliver frosted bottles
of white ice to classmates.

Summer bottles held cocktails of curds,
the stench of which caused heaving seas
of bile in twenty stomachs.

After seeing the nurse we became
pencil monitors and ruler monitors.
Nowadays they have computer monitors.

This is recalled in the brimming dark of Ward 49,
the bleak pre-winter night outside fireflied
with helicopters full of offshore orderlies
rushing to take the pulse of a rig.

Beyond ward windows moonlight caresses lovers,
pulls back their blankets of darkness. Couples blushed
and flushed with sex glow in their cocoons of health.

They are miles and years away from me but I sense
them out there, record their pulsing desires.

Tonight I am the Heart Monitor.

Running Out of World

The man in the bed next door
had a visit from his specialist.

Later that afternoon he got out of bed,
grabbed his stick and went for a short
breathless walk.

*Isn't it great to get out of this room
and back in the world?* I said.

It won't be for long, he replied.

The Only Way Out

He's waiting for his biopsy results.

He leans over and tells me:
I'm on my way out.

You're going home?

No.

He makes the sign of the cross.

Hard to Swallow

I've got bad news for you.
> *Here's the lunch menu...*

The cancer is widespread.
> *Soup with croutons for starters*

We've found lumps everywhere.
> *then meatballs*

In your throat.
> *with sprouts*

In your kidneys.
> *and peas*

In your prostate.
> *or sweetcorn*

You've got small-cell lung cancer.
> *with potatoes.*

I'm afraid it's untreatable.
> *Treacle pudding*

We'll make you as comfortable as possible.
> *with custard.*

Sorry.
> *Or jelly?*
> *Everyone loves the jelly.*

(Author's note— this is near-verbatim reportage of an actual incident. The man in the bed next to mine was being given his biopsy results for everyone to hear whilst a nurse was shouting out the lunch menu to the other patients in the ward.)

If You See a Man

If you see a man weeping,
hold his hand.

If you see a man mourning,
hold his hand.

If you see a man mourning himself,
hold his hand.

If you see a man without hope,
hold his hand.

If you see a man asking for his family,
hold his hand.

If you see a man's wife holding his hand,
she will hold your hand in turn.

And you will be part of their family
until the curtains are drawn.

What They Say About You

Word for Windows

On the estate where I grew up
we didn't have neighbours,
we had witnesses.

And though we weren't unkind,
we robbed each other blind.

Some divvy stole my bike,
so I nicked someone else's.
It was a kind of bartering—
stealing like-for-like.

All through my adolescence
I learnt about the essence of living—
it's a game of give-and-take,
so I gave as good as I got.

The word on the street was
GIVE WAY
so I gave way, but I didn't give in.

We were at that awkward age between
puberty and the pub, between
hopscotch and Scotch on the rocks.

Although our diction seldom stretched
to triple syllables, our tongues were razors
that rendered language blunt.
Rozzers, teachers, neighbours bore the brunt.

If we gave our word we'd batter you,
our word was good.

And we had a word for windows—
that word was *wood*.

Liverpool Echoes

Passing an alley in a foreign town,
the wind seems to whistle a shanty.
A tang of salt coats my tongue.

A building looks the image of
the Bluecoat Chambers. I spot
an Adelphi, a Gambier, a Goree.

A dockside crane wire twangs
that first wild chord of *A Hard Day's
Night* and kick-starts my heart.

A poster shows a Matador razor-
sharp inside the swirl of his cape.

I recall a man in a pub saying:
*Your father must have been hard
as nails to grow up in The Bullring
tenements, son. They were brutal.*

My futile attempt at a foreign phrase
brings whoops of laughter: now that's
the language I learned from my father

when the Hit Parade played on the radio,
the big ship sailed down the alley alley-o
and the Sons of Spion sang *ee-aye-addio:*

when I played football with Rory Storm
as Astrid Kirchherr shot the Beatles
in a basement on the Reeperbahn,

while the Quarrymen laboured at the rock face
of their ordinary lives, and *that mad bastard* Lennon
was let loose amongst the footlights and the headlines.

Notes From the Hurrying Man
for Brian Patten

I might have brushed against you, coming out of Blacklers,
where Pete Best's mother, Mona, bought him his first drum kit.
You, fresh from the Kardomah, seeking out a scarf to shield
you from the winter weather.

I might have brushed against the book of poems in your hand:
may have heard the distant howl of Ginsberg from L.A., or
faintly glimpsed the city lights that shone on Ferlinghetti,
garaging his car in a downbeat Frisco low rise.

You sipped your Kasbah coffee with the icons of the Sixties.
I went to Kirkby Tech along with other factory fodder. I spent
that decade dwarming in a muddled fug. The years spun out
like swarf, swift and jagged from my Boxford.

Yet thirty years later we shared a pint of blether: talked about
your mother, talked about my father and the closing down of
Blacklers. Then we stepped into the future: me to my *Republic*,
you to your *Armada*.

Death Shall Have No Dim Onion

Shopping by woods this snowy eve,
I wonder why each word I read
gets muddled up, goes quite mad.
How did my eyesight get so bad?

Did Robert Browsing's Duchess go
not Gentile Into That Good Night?
Was Robert Frosty in the snow?
Is 'Tyger Tyger *burping*' right?

Poor Percy Shelley's really Pysshe
and Homer wrote the *Ilibad*.
Could Morgenstern recite his *Fish*?
Are Vasco Popadoms a fad?

Once Allen Ginseng's primal *Owl*
drowned out the waving Stevie Sniff.
Hiya, Watha! makes me scowl
like Ruddy Kipling's iffy *If*.

Of all the joys of Muddle Age
myopia must head the queue.
I have to squint to read this page—
The Raver (Edgar Allen Poo).

In Place of Poems

I recall my teacher asking the class
to write a poem about one of their relatives,
then for homework paint a picture of that person.
She called the lesson *Show and Tell*.

I dipped my nib in the inkwell, scrawled
a spiderweb of lines, then blotted my copybook.
At home I coloured in a drawing of my dad
going to work on his bike, sandwiches in his saddlebag.

Tonight, I'll step outside this page and hand to you
items that stood for poems in his world—
a *Football Echo*, bicycle clips, a clock-in card;
a freshly-machined cog dripping with soluble oil.

Genesis & Tinnitus

In The Beginning
was the First Word.

A man heard it.

In The End
was the Last Word.

A woman had it.

Because I am a Poet

I didn't wake at the clock's alarm.
I waited for the glorious dawn
to shake the shackles of sleep from my wrists.

At breakfast I weighed the Sugar Puffs
against the bacon, but opted for the irony
of scrambled eggs and chicken soup.

After calculating the centre of gravity
of the rainbow outside my window, I devised
a formula for finding the avoirdupois mass
of any given teardrop.

Whilst doodling in the margins of a poem
by Wislawa Szymborska I recalled how once
I divined the alchemy of loss on your lips,
sharp as styptic on my tongue,
and fell in love with the Polish word
STĘSKNIONY.

Because I am a poet I know what rhymes
with *Oranjeboom*. I know the precise
chemical composition of Love Hearts.

I also know what *onomatopoeia*, *dénouement*
and *oxymoronic* mean, though I seldom use them
more than once in any given haiku.

After an evening training young verses
how to find their own voices, I stalk moonlit
paths into deep dark woods to recapture
fierce feral poems and herd them home
to their paper cages.

The Downside of Knowing a Poet

Don't write.

Don't phone.

Don't wait
outside my door in the rain.

Yes, I adore you.
I'd do anything for you,

except ever see you again.

Your sorrow
is so tangible
I can taste it,

but our last parting
was so perfect,
it would be a shame to waste it.

On Your Radio Tonight

Musicians are the world's timekeepers.
They're awake for all of late p.m. and early-middle a.m.

They invented, rented, syncopated time. In fact,
they own time, loaning it to our ears chord by chord.

Some would say they own our tears, conjuring
the moistness of memories with a single note.

Others would call them tyrants for invoking
the bliss of loss with a single stroke of a string.

Sneaking up on you, one will blow a note
of such melancholy it turns your heart to jelly.

They're the strummers, the drummers, the blowers:
we're the suckers for every plucker.

Dynamite to broken hearts, they sharpen solitude
to a needlepoint stuck in the vinyl groove of the past.

Turn the dial to left or right, there's no safe songs
on your radio tonight.

Wife of Pi

3.141592
but you don't stop there do you?

caring

nothing for brain cells burning
you greedy little sod (sorry for

swearing)

you've been to every decimal
place on Earth

deterring

other roaming numerals from

daring

you've grown too big
for your roots

inferring

someone ought to knock you
down a peg or two

recurring.

Henri Rousseau Meets Frank O'Hara

It's a jungle out there, Frank.

I know, Henri. Was it you who brought
all this humid weather over from Brooklyn?

There are tigers roaming Central
Park. Don't go there at night without
a flashlight, a pitchfork and a net.

They say you left a naked girl
on a divan, smack in the middle
by that phallic obelisk, you brute.

Don't worry about the girl, Frank,
the saucer-eyed lions look after her.
Say, how long is your lunch break?

It's fluid as a Dali dial, Henri. Museums
have their midday naps. Hell, all that
time they cram in between the entrances

and exits. Nobody's clock-watching
in Antiquities. You fancy a papaya
and a jambalaya from Juliet's Corner?

Papaya? Jungle juice sounds just up
my street. I'd like to do you in oils, Frank,
peeking through a bush on Seventh Avenue.

The Electrode Less Travelled

The tall blonde Swedish girl points to my trousers
and orders: *Get Them Off!* So I get them off.

I am told to lie down and think of Ulrika.
(She doesn't really say that but it's what I do.)

She sticks needles up and down my legs.
I have to compare each tiny pain to every other.

I'm wired with electrodes that send electric pulses
from the nerves in my feet, up my spine and back again.

If I shock you too much you can sue me for abuse –
so shout when the pain becomes unbearable.

I check that her badge reads NHS NEUROLOGY,
not GUANTANAMO BAY RENDITION CENTRE.

The readings I'm getting seem to suggest that
there might be an underlying non-neurological problem.
I think you will need to see your doctor for a blood test.
Also, it will help if you provide a urine sample.

I mull this over.

Let me get this straight – you're getting on my nerves
and now you want my doctor to take the piss?

So, what's left for my friends to do?

Out of the Blue

A dead hawk's ruby fluids poured
in dwindling streams across the moor.

In turmoil from the sky it bowled,
a heart too grave for air to hold.

A long shriek where the hawk had swooned.
A beak had burst the day's balloon.

A figure with a rifle stooped
to nail that last unruly swoop.

Forfeit

You forfeited your life the night you left
the sleeping family that you could not face.
And now: the triumph of a suitcase
at your feet as you try to thumb a lift.

Then headlights turn your way, the evening's gift
is an Eddie Stobart heading for the coast.
You talk but see the driver isn't fussed,
so you count all the hurts that caused the rift.

You're counting all the hurts that caused the rift:
the brief affairs, the drudge, the way she fussed;
the joyless holidays on some grim coast,
the children, matrimony's only gift.

Then suddenly a screech, you feel the lift
of an impact buckling your suitcase
and shattered glass embedding in your face.
You forfeited your life the night you left.

The Lung Launderette

Waiting in the Pulmonary Function Suite
for my Myocardial Perfusion Scan,
I see the nurse clip my chest X-Ray
to a piece of string straddling a light box.

Gawping for ages, I try to decipher
the bar code of my ribs, the stacked cups
of my spine. And what of that grey nebula
hubbled in my pectus like a lethal gas?

I hold a spirit-level to it. Hang a plumb
line off it. Take a light-meter reading.
Spit on a Kleenex and rub, grab a brush
and scrub the smudge with Daz.

Speaking to my doctor a week later, he says
I'll have to retake the test; that cloudy
area was an error due to insufficient radiation
and not, as first suspected, something sinister.

I cancel the headstone carver,
inform the Minister.

Pantoum of the Opera

Is this one *Wagner's Ring?*
There's a cycle in it somewhere.
We'll know the show is over
when the Fat Lady sings.

There's a cycle in it somewhere,
and the Nibelungen Ring.
When the Fat Lady sings
we'll drive to Götterdämmerung

down the Nibelungen ring road.
In a Norbert Dentressangle truck
we'll drive to Götterdämmerung.
Valkyries check their Vodafones

in a Norbert Dentressangle truck.
We'll know the show is over when
Valkyries check their Vodafones:
is this tone Wagner's ring?

Wing Nut

This is a nut with knobs on:
a Mickey Mouse mimic,
confined to comic spirals.
Up and Down
are not in its diction,
they are functions
of circum-
locution.

It moves by rule
of thumb;
a twisted butterfly
fluttering on
unflappable
wings.

Flower Girls

There were days when my father took me to town
to see the circus of the streets: hawkers, market stalls
and my aunties, the Flower Girls of Williamson Square.

They peeked like petunias from under their scarves,
wore shy smiles against the wind, fingered flowers through
sawn-off mittens, pocketed pennies, tanners and florins.

Then we wandered through fog to the Pier Head,
a vastness of slabs where slaves once shuffled
in chain-linked lines for auction in the Confederate States.

We came in saner times to see a white man in chains,
for amusement, not enslavement. Shackled head to foot,
upside-down in a sack, he won his freedom in seconds flat.

This was childhood folklore: the ghosts of Speke Hall,
the Childe of Hale, who was nine feet tall, the Witches
of Pendle: spectres that drove you to bolt your door.

And over my shoulder, some thirty miles eastwards,
a girl *The Echo* described as *vivacious* met someone
called Myra whilst picking flowers on Saddleworth Moor.

A Perfect Poem

Look, I'm sorry.
I know I promised you a poem,
a perfect poem, on this very page.
It was here this morning.
But it's gone now.
Gone.

You would have loved it.
All the letters were heart-shaped
and the words were so tender
they looked like silver tears.
The page itself would tremble
like a handkerchief waving goodbye,

but the poem had teeth.
It was a sassy little number,
a street-wise, sardonic piece
with wit so sharp I cut my fingers
to shreds just writing it,

but it was ambitious,
and though it knew I loved it dearly,
no page of mine could ever hold it.

It wanted to be a star of TV.
Wanted to be published in anthologies,
to be set-reading for GCSEs,
be translated into Japanese,
and be read aloud by famous tongues
on *Poetry Please.*

The last time I saw it,
it had had enough.

This morning
as I was leaving to meet you
I passed it in the hallway.
It was on the phone
to Roger McGough.

Kenneth's Father's Canine Is Deceased

Ken Dodd's Dad's Dog's Dead.

Dodd's Dog's Dead, Ken? —Dad.

Dad Dodd's Dog's Dead —Ken.

Dog's Dead? —Ken Dodd's Dad.

Dead— Ken Dodd's Dad's Dog.

What They Say About You

They say that you'll be leaving me tonight.
I'm weary with remorse and loss of sleep.
I weep for all the things I can't put right.

The words we had were bitter, cutting deep,
my shamed, averted eyes stare at the floor,
you gesture with a tired, dismissive sweep.

You seem to be more distant than before—
a door to somewhere else now holds your gaze.
I raise my voice to supplicate, implore

for one more chance, a few forgiving days.
I touch your face and kiss a last goodnight.
The light is dimmed, the nurses walk away.

They say that you'll be leaving me tonight.

Indelible

Weeks after the wake,
my first dream of you.

You're standing at the rails of a ship
on a clear blue day, sailing on that huge
Cunarder we used to watch from the Floating
Dock; decked out for a breezy jamboree,
floating towards an improbable country.

From your stillness you turn to me, say nothing,
but your eyes speak of fair weather and calm waters.

As the eighth bell tolls I leave you there
and swim back to wakefulness, viewing your
vast indelible smile from my far impossible shore.

Consolations

The first week over, I said to my sister:
Before we know it, it'll be a year.

Then we'll be placing anniversary flowers
in the garden of his memory.

Meanwhile, there's refuge in things
beyond his compass;

I drive to work, knowing full well
that his hands never held a steering wheel,

or sit at my computer, knowing he never
caressed a keyboard with his fingers.

I have come to know the small consolations
of technology:

mobile phones, e-mails, DVDs—
all safe from any taint of melancholy,

but football scores, gunfighter ballads,
darts, snooker, the *Grand Ole Opry*,

that's a different story.

In the Other Dole Queue

I spot Yosser Hughes,
so I call to him —

Hey, Yosser!
What's it feel like
to be a fictional character?

Yosser shouts back —
I'm made up!

The Uptake

I figured it was over
when you didn't phone
for years on end.

The End of Poetry

One of the secret powers of this poem
is to render the reader's clothing invisible.

This may account for the occasional
cries of alarm heard in Public Libraries.

So be careful where you read these words.
And next time you see someone bare

and oblivious in a bookshop, stay calm.
Close the book and lead them gently

from the Poetry shelves, avoiding
the Children's section, and usher them

to the *Meet-the-Author* stand, where they will
join others to form a nude tableau entitled:

*Reading Poetry Is Like Standing Naked In Front
Of People And Baring Your Soul To Them.*

Let them become aware of each other's bodies.
Let them begin where all poems end.

New Poems

Ringo Starry Rhymes

At the present moment, Liverpool is the centre of the consciousness of the human universe.
—Allen Ginsberg, 1965

Ginsberg walks down Mathew Street, home to *the minstrels of Cavernsink.* The path his sandals tread is his Mersey beat: the Haight-Ashbury & Greenwich Village of the Brits. The zeitgeist jives in the stellar cellar city down below these streets: he can feel the boom joy with his feet, almost taste the twang tang of guitars, smell the high octane of hairsprayed Beehives & reefer rauch wafting from that underground of sound: shaken, rattled & rolled by groups of local kids in Cuban Heels, up for anything that reeks of booze & sex & drugs: those blue remembered pills. Beat music, Beat city: Corso's preaching counter-culture to a bunch of *whatthehellisheonabout?* faces in Crosby Library; Kerouac's scattering poems on the road out to Kirkby & Larry Ferlinghetti's giving it laldy in Fazakerley. They turn their ampersands up loud & begin to bray. Allen's hit town too early for *The Entry of Christ Into Liverpool*, so he sips a catholic cocktail with a twist of Lime Street and a slice of Lennon in the holy disco light of the wigwam cathedral. Now he's howling with the clubbers behind the Iron Door & Peppermint Lounge, playing song-sticks in the Sink & chinging finger-cymbals in the Pink Flamingo. He's chanting Vedas in the Philharmonic bar: *Tat Tvam Asi, Tat Tvam Asi, Thou Art That, Thou Art That, Wack.* He hums the Morning Ragas in the Mission Home for Sailors, then hollers out Upanishads up Upper Parley from a Corporation OMnibus. He quotes the *Bhagavad Gita* in the Penny Lane bus shelter. When he speaks about Arjuna, everyone thinks that's his brother. After Brian, Adrian & Roger speak their Ringo Starry rhymes they have the craic in Ye Olde Cracke & stay for the after-hours, under-the-counter-culture: Rizla-skinned rollies jazzed with juju weed — all a poet needs after a hard day's rant.

Swarfega

Washing off marking blue with the green jelly
of Swarfega, I think of my father doing the same
after each shift half a century ago; his orange
overalls smeared black with grease and oil,
his hair greased back with Brylcreem,
and for a moment my right hand is his
right hand washing my left. I clasp
to hold him there but my hands slip apart
and leave me standing, open armed,
like a man about to embrace a ghost.

Borderline

I looked to the streets, the bars, the Bingo halls;
the Legion, the betting shop, the fields
of Anfield Road.

I listened for a solitary voice
in the massed throng of the Kop.

I watched the Mersey ferry its freight
of enterprise, musicianship and fellowship
to the far Americas.

I heard the echoes of small, burdened footsteps
trudging five aching miles as my 10-year-old father
carried his dying brother to the hospital.

Then, as daylight faded, I heard from the river
a murmur of one man talking
and many more laughing,

and I knew I'd reached the borders
of the Republic of Ted.

Long Ago With Giacomo.

Born to a wealthy Lombardy family,
Agostini rode for Morini
when Tarquinio Provini
left to ride for Benelli.

His friend, Gilberto Parlotti,
rode for Tomos and Derbi,
and died on a Morbidelli.

Agostini rode MVAugusta
against the Redman Honda
in the Japanese town of Suzuka.

He whirred in his blur in front
of me and Hailwood at Glen Helen:
Mike the Bike and *Ago*
on their scalding oil machines.

Those days my father worked
at the Halewood Assembly.
The words he used were *Divvy,
Doolally* and *Antwacky.*

Back in the ramshackle factory,
I became quietly exotic, having
learned the Latin roots
of *acceleration* and *velocity*
at the 1967 Isle of Man TT.

Supine

This landscape enlivens us;
dispels dullness, quells our sullen pinings.

Advancing up elliptical paths,
seeking unseen lupine or vulpine tracks
above the pine line, we line-up lenses like snipers
to capture eagles and their prey in spinning duels.

Canvas advances into the wilderness.
Supine, I prime your newly-ginned lips,
click open clasps. Outside, the moon blushes
at our pulsing orange shadows.

Rosacea

If a face is a rose, it draws thorns
and barbs from ignorant mouths
making wine-stain and port-storm
alcoholic accusations.

If a face is a flame, it's a burning blush.
Roseate skin is another wall,
a border post, a further division
for those who see no deeper than cells.

A red rag to to a bully,
it's a hide hung out in raw winds;
what's left when you strip the pelt
of the word *flay* from your thesaurus.

Life is Like a Dragonfly

days drag
&
years fly

Seaside Chinos

Christmas:
a chain of hollies
from Sauchiehall
to Suilven.

Hailstones echo
in this high shoal of mist.
Snow shines lilac.
I inhale loch airs.

Sunflares track the loci
of my lens which seeks
the distant ice-haloed isles.

I must be insane
to be climbing in seaside
chinos – scant defence against
a rapscallion wind's ashen chill.

Removing my half-inch soles,
rubbing lichen oils into my toes,
I calculate the cosine
of each mountain slope,
divine the ache of each hill.

Having chiselled my name
into Scottish rock, I abandon
these chastening heights
for oceans and canoes.

I descend to a chorus
of Noels and Halleluiahs.

Scan

Your head is strapped to a metal scoop.
One ton of scanner lowers towards you.
A cross enlarges from its centre until
the screen touches the tip of your nose.
Ask yourself if you really believe
the machine will stop there.
Come to know the true meaning of faith.

Question and Answer

I sit on my mat and pray to the Lord
to end my days in the sweetness of home,
far from this place that has no name for love.
Whatever the question, the answer is blood.

My life was a kite but now it's a stone.
My hands are held fast, my skull is a cave.
Each day the footsteps come down from above.
Whatever the question, the answer is blood.

This darkness is constant, my thoughts are grave.
Each minute is vast, an infinite dome.
I dreamt of a hawk devouring a dove.
Whatever the question, the answer is blood.

The days of the world have raged and moved on:
my wife is now old, the children have grown.
I raised my voice, met a fist in a glove.
Whatever his question, my answer is blood.

Tom Waits Meets Liberace

My piano's in rehab. My voice is employed
by NASA to check for Shuttle tile vibration.
There are twenty-four variations of *mule*.

George does all the donkey work while I dress up
for my act. I wear my costumes the way cardinals do.
The Church was the earliest form of show business.

Jesus's cross wasn't studded with rhinestones, you know.
There were no candelabras at Calvary. Did I tell you that
Swordfishtrombones rearranges to Downshift Sombreros?

I was on Oprah Winfrey once. Not literally, of course.
I called her by her reverse name, Harpo. *She wasn't*
amused. Were you ever on the Muppet Show, Tom?

No. I've been on Letterman, though. I told him that
my next European concert would be in Formaldehyde,
a suburb of Dublin, on the *Glitter & Gloom* tour, 2008.

Glitter? Do I detect my influence there? I'm flattered.
What mattered always was my music. Am I one of the greats,
the heir of Liszt? I think I know. What's your legacy?

"Fast, Cheap and Good. Pick two. If it's fast and cheap
it won't be good. If it's cheap and good it won't be fast.
If it's fast and good it won't be cheap." Words to live by.

The word "cheap" was choked by my cheque book years ago.
I know what they say about me. They have the cheek to call
ME trash. But THEY don't look good in hotpants, the peasants.

Red pants on a powder-blue night is more my bag, Lee.
Did you ever wear a pork pie hat? You know, the problem
for an audience is they've never worked together before.

I'm a mix, Tom – Italian/Polish. We were poor in both
languages. I've known hard times, but not with women.
I never married. Why? Speculate at your ease while
I put on my favourite Law Suit.

If you wanna stop chicks, play *Chopsticks*. Let *them* wear
the lipstick. See, you and me, we're easing into musical
history. We got to get behind the Muse in the morning
and plough.

So It Goes

What we had,
all that was,
is no more.

Down to dust
went the hours
of each year.

Not one sign
of what we
were is left.

Those who are
yet to come
will not know

why we ached
for him or
longed for her.

Or how, in
all our days,
no love came.

Asbohemian Rhapsody

See him, over there in the Poetry Section,
hunched over a selection of Anne Sexton?

He's the Local Poet.

They say what he lacks in looks and verve
he makes up for with sheer nerve at Open
Mics, where he reads the poetic equivalent
of the quest for the final digit of pi.
Compounding this delight, all his lines begin with

I.

He's been given an Arts Council Asbo for this,
and three months' hard labour in a remedial poetry
workshop where he's forced to break up difficult
second-hand words and forge them into new
coinage: constructing owls from verbs and vowels,
whole towns from concrete nouns.

The Pope Has No Truck

When buying a relic or an icon from the Vatican,
say a phial of stigmata from some martyr or other,
do nothing as drastic as flashing the plastic—
the Pope has no truck with Maestro or Visa
for anything cheaper than a Pietà.

When purchasing from dioceses, pay in the manner
that pleases *The Boss in Rome*— he tops up the credit
on his Popemobile phone, renews his subscription
to *The Wholly Buyable* and acquires his beatific bling
with only one thing—

When in Rome be sure to remember the jingle—
For all purchases Papal, pay by Pray Pal.

Inundating
for and after Todd McEwen.

There's a woman in a state outside the Empire
State. Someone cries for her outside the Chrysler,
but she cannot hear him sobbing.

A girl is blubbing in the Guggenheim,
drowning in saltwater. A man's beside
himself inside the Lyric Diner. An artist
is weeping on the steps outside of MoMA.

All along the gridded streets, all along
the avenues, are lines of bawling lovers:
the damp, the moist, the downright drenched
watch their hearts swill down the sewers.

Rain pelts into every pore, pours down
town like fleets of sodden buses.
It's cold enough to snow, cold enough to hail

a yellow cab to anywhere. Uptown sluices
Downtown. Lexington's a lake.
Subway steps run riverlike.
The Battery's a dyke.

Underground, it's Dante's Deluge;
a watery hell. Shoes bloat and swell.
A flood of mascara runs.
Coats weigh tons.

The A train's a kayak.
The B train's all at sea.
The D train drains itself
of passengers on Es.

The F expels in waterfalls, in torrents
of defeat: slops its carriageloads
of heartbreak onto Bleecker Street.

Understanding Poetry

Whose woods these are I think I know.
Greg Norman finds some lost golf clubs.

You do not do any more black shoe.
Imelda Marcos has a hissy fit.

Hope is the thing with feathers.
Icarus gets it wrong again.

Tiger, tiger, burning bright.
Barbecue time at London Zoo.

La Belle Dame Sans Mersey.
Keats' bird leaves Liverpool.

How do I love thee? Let me count the ways.
Elizabeth Barrett Browning discovers the *Kama Sutra*.

Water, water, everywhere, and all the boards did shrink.
Coleridge phones the emergency plumber.

Half a league, half a league, half a league onwards.
The effect of three points early in the season.

Once upon a midnight dreary.
New Year's Eve isn't what it used to be.

By the shore of Gitche Gumee, by the shining Big-Sea-Water.
Yet again, Longfellow forgets the word 'lake.'

The curfew tolls the knell of parting day.
How to keep the London rioters at bay.

Look at the pictures and the cutlery.
The music in the piano stool. That vase.
Philip Larkin has a garage sale.

The force that through the green fuse drives the flower.
Dylan Thomas gets the wiring wrong.

I sing the body electric.
So does Walt Whitman.